Armless
Hugs

OTHER BOOKS BY JIM MEEHAN

Hearts Have Reasons
(UK Outword Trust 1995; USA Thomas Moor 2000)

Reasons Have Hearts Too
(UK Outword Trust 1997; USA Thomas Moore 2000)

Sugar Free Sweet Talk
(USA Talent Plus 2009)

Hallways to Success and Significance
(USA Talent Plus 2013)

I Mean You No Harm; I Seek Your Greatest Good –
Reflections on Trust (USA I Universe 2015)

Armless

JIM MEEHAN

ARMLESS HUGS

iUniverse books may be ordered through booksellers or by contacting:

iUniverse
1663 Liberty Drive
Bloomington, IN 47403
www.iuniverse.com
844-349-9409

Because of the dynamic nature of the Internet, any web addresses or links contained in this book may have changed since publication and may no longer be valid. The views expressed in this work are solely those of the author and do not necessarily reflect the views of the publisher, and the publisher hereby disclaims any responsibility for them.

Any people depicted in stock imagery provided by Getty Images are models, and such images are being used for illustrative purposes only. Certain stock imagery © Getty Images.

ISBN: 978-1-6632-0743-2 (sc)
ISBN: 978-1-6632-0744-9 (e)

Print information available on the last page.

iUniverse rev. date: 06/08/2023

To
All those people helping others infected with
or vulnerable to the coronavirus

Many thanks and armless hugs.

Contents

Preface

Like millions of people all over the world, Maureen, my wife, Larissa, my daughter, Amir my grandson and yours truly have been in lockdown for a couple of months. Every Thursday evening at eight o'clock, here in the UK, we have an event called 'clap for carers.' We go into our front garden, clap our hands, blow whistles, and make a racket on home-made drums in recognition and appreciation of the sacrifices being made by employees of our National Health Service and others who are putting their lives at risk to save lives and protect those who are vulnerable to the coronavirus.

During this lockdown period Bob Attwood a good friend and a member of our rambling club SWALLOWS II (Short Walks And Long Lunches On WednesdayS) asked if my poem *Armless Hugs* written in July 1997 could be seen as a premonition of current times. Although I assured him that it was not meant to be I also told him that I got his point which was made with the benefit of twenty – twenty vision, as it were. Who could have envisioned twenty three years ago that so many people would only be able to hug their loved ones with their hands by their sides as they were physically isolated from them even at the time of their death?

Following this conversation my mind turned back to 1997 and recalled how the poem came about. I was putting together a collection of verse for my mother's eightieth birthday which fell in December of that year. At the time my professional work as a positive psychologist and an international leadership consultant meant that

I had to travel worldwide. Often I returned home to the United Kingdom in the middle of the night or in the early hours of the morning. I remember popping into our bedroom to see my wife, Maureen, sound asleep and then checking on my daughter, Larissa who was also in the 'land of nod.' On such occasions I was overcome by a strong positive feeling tinged with some regret; on the one hand I wanted to engage them and on the other hand appreciated they needed the benefits of a good night's sleep. I could not put these feelings into words and would retire to sleep in the spare bedroom. The same sensations arose when I made phone calls to them from abroad but again I failed to capture the feelings in words.

Then something unusual happened. In July 1997 I was analyzing the transcript of a telephone interview of the chief executive of a Canadian ski resort which was also playing on an audio tape. He talked fast and had a strong French twang in his voice. When describing how he evaluated the discipline he received as a child, which he saw as pretty positive, he added, "It's a challenge when bringing up, you know, bringing up children on how to sort of, how to **hug them with your arms by your side**. I don't know if that explains it or not." Stunned, I dropped my pen on hearing those words as they encapsulated precisely the feelings I could not put into words. His words had struck a chord in me and for several weeks swirled around in my head eventually emerging in the form of a poem entitled *Armless Hugs*.

By the year 2000 Maureen and I were living in Lincoln, Nebraska in the United States and an American firm arranged to publish my first two books of poems. As part of the promotion of the books I appeared on television (ABC Channel 8) and at the end of an interview was asked to recite a poem of my choice. I chose *Armless Hugs*.

The subsequent reaction to the TV show was positively overwhelming. Some of the messages I received ended with the words 'Armless hugs' rather than with 'best wishes' or other closures. Accordingly, when writing to some family members and close friends

I started using the words to close my correspondence. Several people asked if I used the title *Armless Hugs* because it sounded like harmless hugs. There was no conscious intention on my part but the association makes a lot of sense. Interestingly the connection is even more relevant today as the phrase "do no harm" was attributed to the famous Greek physician Hippocrates (460 BCE to375 BCE) the Father of Medicine. Even today many doctors sign a version of the Hippocratic Oath which has become an ethical principle or rule of behavior. So we are thanking our carers for doing no harm to others when we clap for them each Thursday evening. For me there is another strange coincidence in this connection to Hippocrates. Recently I learned that Hippocrates died in Larissa, Greece. Maureen and I were totally unaware of this fact when we named our daughter Larissa.

Although I retired as a practicing positive psychologist and international leadership consultant in 2015 I am still pursuing areas of interest in science. Maureen, my wife and I returned to the United Kingdom to be closer to our daughter, Larissa and our grandson Amir. Dabbling in rhyming verse has been a lifetime hobby and continues to this day.

However, Bob Attwood's chance conversation prompted me to review my previous poetic work. It had become obvious to me that some of my poems did not reflect my current perspective and it was time to put together an up to date collection. Some poems have been discarded, some remain unaltered, some have been revised and a few new ones have been added. It seemed appropriate to call the resultant collection *Armless Hugs*. The poems in Part One are focused on human relationships while those in Part Two are more general in their scope. Opposite some poems there are footnotes providing relevant contextual information.

My hope is that you will find some items enjoyable and thought provoking.

Jim Meehan
June 30th 2020

I've learned that people will forget
what you said, people will forget
what you did, but people will never forget
how you made them feel.

Maya Angelou

Do all you can,
With what you have,
In the time you have,
In the place you are.

Nykosi Johnson

PART ONE

Relationships

Armless Hugs

Seeing you there sleeping, I swell with pride.
At such times I've learned to hug you with my arms by my side.

When far away from you travelling world-wide,
On the phone I've learned to hug you with my arms by my side.

Even in your company, my true feelings can sometimes be denied,
Leaving me hugging you with my arms by my side.

I realise I'm not always fooling you when I try to hide my real
feelings inside.
Your smiles and laughter my guilt override…................
……................and I'm drawn to your arms which are always
open wide.

Enough is Enough

You have always been my enough.
I never expected you to be perfect.
People are not made of such sweet stuff,
In function and form free from defect.

Thank you for accepting me as your enough.
For allowing me to sometimes get it wrong.
For selectively calling my bluff,
Whenever my dance did not match my song.

Empathy

If we could listen actively to our every word and sigh,
Would I see you, as you do, and you me as I?

If we could watch each other carefully, when we laugh and cry,
Would I feel, as you feel, and you sense as I?

If we could walk in each other's shoes and not be passers-by,
Would I see the world as you do, and you the world as I?

Active listening and self-disclosure will lead by and by,
To a deeper understanding – seeing more than eye to eye

Total Mutual Trust

I mean you no harm;
I seek your greatest good.
Come take me by the palm,
We'll see the stars not just the mud.
We'll adopt a more positive role,
We'll walk that extra mile.
We'll see the parts and the whole,
No longer half dead, but fully alive.

I mean you no harm;
I seek your greatest good.
Come take me by the arm.
We'll understand and then be understood.
We'll find ourselves in each other.
And lose ourselves there too.
The mystery of "I" – "Other,"
One entity, yet two.

I mean you no harm;
I seek your greatest good,
In cold weather I'll keep you warm.
When hungry I'll give you food.
My life is filled with calm,
As it is fully understood,
Yes…
You mean me no harm,
You seek my greatest good

This poem was inspired by the idea of a verbal love cup. The words slide down from the inner lip to the base which has ... That longing...inscribed on it before climbing up the opposite side from base to inner lip.

Belonging

What you and I have is something very special.
You know what I mean.
That longing when you're not here.
That longing when you are near.
That longing night and day.
That longing to hear what you say.
That longing to feel your touch…

…That longing…

That longing to give you so much.
That longing that you hear what I say.
That longing that won't go away.
That longing when you are near.
That longing when you are not here.
You know what I mean.
What you and I have is something very special.

Lost and Found

Let us lose ourselves once more in love tonight,
Explore a life of bliss and put our cares to flight.
Let us completely relax and take our time,
And taste a drop of deep red wine.

Let us find ourselves once more in love tonight,
Lift the blinds that mar the moment of clear insight.
Let us become more open and thus enable,
Truth to replace what is false, fact what is fable.

Empathy or Sympathy

"Your wounds deeply wound me."
Emotional empathy mainly.

"You have my pity."
Sympathy to a high degree.

"Your situation is clear to me."
Rational empathy mostly.

"I wouldn't do that if I were you."
Neither of the two.

"I feel your pain."
Emotional empathy again.

"I know that you know I try to see the way you see it,
And try to feel it the way you feel it,
And that I will help you in any way I can."

Now that's total empathy man!

This poem is based on words contained in Julian Barnes book "The Levels of Life." Section three "The Loss of Depth."

Missing You

You are the heart of my life and the life of my heart.
Missing you is the pain of being apart.

The more it hurts
The more love's worth.

If it didn't matter.
It wouldn't matter.

You are the heart of my life and the life of my heart.
Missing you is the pain of being apart.

Love Donors

Love donors seek another's greatest good.
Love is in their blood.

We soon discover
Their love group is "positive other."

Love donors we need to be,
Transfusing charity.

When a party, not a funeral is going on inside
Then joy to others we can provide.

If our cup is brimming over
Love cascades to many others.

Growth

Growth begins when blaming ends.
Finger pointing loses many friends.
All good relationships demand,
First finding the root causes of problems at hand.

Solutions not scapegoats need to be the goal,
Pictures change when facts unfold.
Mistakes and errors are not ignored,
Support and tough love see growth restored.

If human faults and failings first come to mind,
Peoples' strengths and beauty are difficult to find.
Growth begins when blaming ends.
Too much criticism loses many friends.

Significance

We all need to feel significant.
It's part of the human predicament.

To give and receive recognition
Improves the human condition.

A loving relationship resulted in most people's birth.
People should be valued not hurt.

So throughout your life ensure you discover
At least one significant other.

Such people will see and bring out the best in you,
And help you to act likewise too.

Love in Words and Numbers

In English you can say it in two – "love you."
You can say it in three – "I love thee."
You can say it in four – "I love you more."
You can say it 'til numbers and words have gone.
But you can't say it in one!

Three's A Crowd

Communication is one of humankind's obsessions.
What is needed is less mass media and more two way, one on one sessions.

Love in Action

Loving others brings out the best in us.
Loving is what loving does.
Investing in others for their sake always results in a hidden return.
If you and I are in some sense one then loving you is loving me in turn.
The effects of altruism and self-interest are the same.
In giving ourselves to others our true selves we gain.
Loving helps us all to grow, but fear and hate diminish us.
Love in action is the way to go to achieve flourishing finishes.

The Lonely World of "I" - "Me"

Some people don't really seem to bother
Living in the world of "I"-"Other."
They really seem content to be
In the lonely world of "I" – "Me."
Only ever saying hello,
To their only companion, their own ego.

The Breath of Life

Without a doubt ......

My body will die if I only breathe in and don't breathe out.

It is indeed also true ...

That I'll die as a person if I think only of me and little of you.

We can also say ...

Life is measured by the number of times our breath is taken away.

Free Flow

It's never too late to relate.
You're never too old to unfold.
Just open your heart,
That'll do for a start,
Let go. Don't try to control.

Trust or Bust

What when absent makes a relationship go bust?
What if not found means a relationship is lost?
What is not only desirable, but also a must?
The cementing ingredient is mutual trust.

Show Your Hand

Babies emerge from the womb into the light,
With fists clenched, locksmith tight.
Let's hope when into their tombs they later slide,
A life of giving has stretched their hands open wide.

Teenagers are Tops

Teenagers are like tops spinning.
Too much parental influence can lead to a fall.
What they need is balanced steering,
To help them keep their eye on the ball.

Obsessed

Steeped in my work or out walking,
I often call you to mind,
And take pleasure in guessing,
Just how you're spending your time.

When lost in a world of ideas,
With my head high in the clouds,
Your face suddenly appears –
Your voice not terribly loud.

When wrapped in the warmth of your body,
With your will welded to mine,
Lovers meant always to be,
For all, yes, all of our time.

Compassion

Your pain and joy in my heart,
This is both a skill and an art.

To really feel what you're going through,
And see how closely I can come to you.

I'll listen actively to what you say
And, non- judgmentally accept all you convey.

I'll do whatever you require,
Your greatest good is all I desire.

Your sorrows I yearn to take away,
And give you some sun in which to make some hay.

The more of you I understand,
The better fashioned is my helping hand.

Another's Shoes

When walking in another's shoes I first must get out of mine.
If I step on another's shoes I must bring out their shine.

About Relating

To relate to others, I have no doubt,
Unless we go within, we'll go without.
Unless we know how we're feeling and what we're thinking about,
Actions' true motivations we'll never fathom out.
Was it a bribe or was it a gift?
Is that certain smile, really a downer with a facelift?
To relate to others I have no doubt,
Unless we go within, we'll go without.

Partial Pictures

Mainly through interactions with others I gradually become me.
From cradle to grave, an amazing mystery.
In the same way others are shaped by these interactions too,
Influencing, imitating, attracting, repelling, are among the things people do.
We never see the total picture when we try to get to know ourselves and others,
But it has never stopped people from becoming true lovers.

Roses in December

I'm glad we've evolved the ability to remember,
So that we, in the North, can have roses in December.
Just think of all the things we might recall,
When in the seasons of our lives we reach the Fall.

Now is the time to fill our memory banks,
By helping others and giving thanks
For the opportunity to do a little good
And collect one more unforgettable rosebud.

Valentine Time

Moments of ecstasy, though timeless, do not last forever.
We must cherish them at the time.
There is much in them to be mindful of, and to savour,
With you my Valentine.

A lifetime compared to infinity may be next to nothing
In the total lapse of time.
Yet intensity in living and loving,
With you is truly sublime.

Moments with you can't be measured by clocks.
It's another sort of time.
It varies in pace and sometimes stops,
Let's enjoy our "Valentine Time."

Making Up

Let me plant a kiss in the place where your tears run dry
And in your arms entwine.
Let me wipe the water from your eyes
And be your Valentine.

Love

Love is not just an emotion or a feeling,
Given to only those who we find appealing.

Love is not manipulating or using,
A game of one winning and one losing.

Love grows by giving it away
Love fades by keeping others at bay.

Love is not selfish or grabbing,
A matter of consuming or having.

Love is a process of relating,
The mysterious interdependence of I – other celebrating.

Love has others as its main focus of concern,
That's when its flame will truly burn.

Counting Some of the Ways

I've lost the note on which you wrote
Something nice - "When I count my blessings I count you twice."
But I often find these words come to mind.
So on this Valentine's Day I would like to say,
In a belated response, "When I count my blessings I count you more than once,
Forever my love with certainty, you can definitely count on me."

There's More

There's more to you than meets the eye,
There's more to tears when you cry.
There's more to you than what you show,
There's more to you than others know.
There's more to words than what is said,
There's more to following than being led.
There's more to kissing than touching lips,
There's more to satire than pointed quips.
There's more to alms than in the giving,
There's more to life than just in living.
There's more to action than the deeds,
There's more to words than what we read.

Beyond Loving

Beyond loving there is no greater thing you can do.
When you're through loving you're through.

PART TWO

General Ideas

A Relative Dimension

Too slow for those that wait,
Stolen by those who procrastinate.

Too swift for those who fear,
Bringing crises ever near.

Too short for those who smile,
Hoping it could linger for a while.

Too long for those who mourn,
Yet it tarries not for anyone.

That which many people try to kill,
Lovers find for them stands still.

Great men leave their footprints on its sands,
We all have it on our hands.

So as it passes, flies or flows,
Make sure you smell many a rose!

Spending Time

You can spend your time wisely or waste it like a fool,
You can never get it back when gone – that's nature's golden rule.
There's fourteen hundred and forty minutes given to everyone every single day,
To sleep, to think, to feel, and much to do and say.
Please whatever you decide don't fritter yours away!

Reality

A blind man and a deaf man walked through a storm,
But their meanings and feelings were not the same.
Different pictures in different frames.

One man's thunder and the other's flashes are just as true.
It is by sharing our pieces that we gain a fuller view.
From partial pictures of me and partial pictures of you.

Smile Inside

Smile inside! Put a stop to that self-pitying sob!
True happiness is, above all else, an inside job.

Attitudes

All attitudes can be reduced to two,
If you take a simplistic view.
Humans can at times be a positive and upbeat force,
or negative and destructive of course.

Humans crave, need, yearn, want and ache.
But they also have to give, not just take.
Humans drive, expand, swell and grow.
But they also have to ebb, not just flow.

What humans are against, the opposite they are for.
It would appear there is a universal law.
To every yes is there a no?
To every con a pro?

But where does indifference fit into this binary code?
Is there not a neutral road,
when at times humans couldn't care less?
Or is this just seen as a lack of positive interest?

Outcomes

A living body gives rise to a living mind.
The two are inextricably combined.

This is not an area of clear black and white.
Deep in the psyche feelings and emotions excite.

Gut reactions could be nut reactions in disguise,
Intuition, polysyllogisms cut down to size.

Impulse, the brains parallel processing gone wild.
Spontaneous creativity, reason's real child.

A living body gives rise to a living mind.
As an engine is to power, likewise is the body to the mind?

Emotion's Parent

Meaning gives birth to emotion, passion is reason's real child.
The mind is a tight or free-reining parent controlling or letting its
child run wild.

Attainment or missing goals plays its part in what we feel.
Understanding our social environment influences what we control
or reveal.

Autumn's Renewal

Is it because Winter nears,
That most trees shed their leafy tears?
Is it because Summer's gone,
That it's no longer warm?
Is it because the trees are tired,
That they can't hold their blooms so long?
Or is it that they require
More fresh sap to keep them strong?

Many birds feel the Fall
As nature's sign to take the air
And answer this instinctive call
To seek warmth and sun elsewhere.
Leaving us behind to stare
At the browns, yellows and gold,
That remind us every year
That we, like trees grow old.

Autumn's a time to take stock of time
And retreat from life's pressures,
To renew rhythm and rhyme
And realize life's treasures.

Autumn signals Winter's cold
And nature slows down its pace.
Shorter days and longer nights unfold,
Less daylight in which to race.

Opposites

When very happy we often cry.
To grow, then to self in part we must die.
Our bodies are changing but we are the same.
All around us is the permanence of change.
Value from suffering often emanates,
Like the perfume from crushed roses or wine from crushed grapes.

A Time Machine

Forward, forward we relentlessly go,
Leaving dates and distance behind.
How remarkable it is to know,
The only way backwards is through the mind.

The mind is the only time machine we possess
To learn lessons to use in the present day.
And thus avoid a previous mess
That needs to remain in yesterday.

A Humanistic Creed

Confused by conflicting claims of religious and philosophical theories,
We search blindly for the meaning of life.
Perhaps the endeavor would reach an earlier conclusion if we abandoned 'isms' and 'ologies.'
And just helped people in their daily strife.
Helping others, liked or not, whatever their need,
Could lead to a meaningful humanistic creed.
One which arises from thinking, feeling and acts of charity,
Mixed according to each person's priority.

Priceless Values

Attention, time and listening draw people near.
Voltaire quipped, "That the best route to the heart was the ear."

By being interested in others we can become their objects of
interest too.
Requiring time together to exchange points of view.

Giving time to others and listening attentively,
Subliminally conveys their value and human dignity.

We underestimate the power of listening more.
By preferring jaw, jaw and yes, more jaw!

"Money can't buy me love," sang the Fab Four.
Love needs something additional that's for sure.

There's one maxim no can one deny.
People value most the things they just can't buy.

Before After Before

Before the storm, the lull.
After empty, full.
Before the fall, the decline.
After clouds, sunshine.
Before after, before.
After uncertain, sure.
Before tears, laughter.
After before, after.
Before joy, pain.
After sun, rain.
Before hope, despair.
After here, there.
Before stop, go.
After to, fro.
Before found, lost.
After free, cost.
Before an up, a down.
After a smile, a frown.
Before go, wait.
After love, hate.
Before happy, sad.
After sane, mad.

Before clean, mess.
After sin, blessed.
Before laugh, weep.
After tired, sleep.
Before war, peace.
After famine, feast.
Before drink, thirst.
After better, worse.
Before lost, keep.
After look, leap.
Before fail, try.
After truth, lie.
Before all, none.
After rain, sun.
Before tall, small.
After rise, fall.
Before lover, friend.
After beginning, end.

Insight

Often when the commonplace is touched by the hand of a genius,
great beauty appears.
Often simplicity lies at the root of humankind's greatest ideas.
Often reality is masked by layers of sophisticated intellectual veneers,
Awaiting an incisive mind to penetrate and clear.

Picture A World

Picture a world where each person was fully employed
In doing good things they were good at, intended and passionately enjoyed!
A place where due recognition was given and people became the best they can,
Significance shining it the eyes of every child, woman and man.

Picture a world where each person was fully engaged
In positively making a difference, whatever their strengths, race, religion or age.
A place where trusting relationships were valued above all.
Welcome to the dreamland of a certain Doctor William E. Hall.

Strength to Strength

Nurture your nature
Your best side of course,
Aces not spaces
Are growth's greatest force.

Invest in strengths and grow
This always gives the best return
Focusing on severe weaknesses is a NO!
Managing around them needs to be learned.

Silk purses from sows' ears are not made,
Put your best jockey on your best horse.
Bolts of silk must be your trade,
Put the right horse on the right course.

Weaknesses do not ignore,
Spectacles help poor eyes.
But strengths need your attention more
That's where the real treasure lies.

Strengths you don't use you'll lose.
Practice, only of a strength, makes perfect.
Others' strengths you can certainly choose,
In place of your serious defects.

All you really need to know,
Is....that if you do more of what you're good at and enjoy, YOUR'E
GUARANTEED TO GROW!

Dr. Hall was my psychological mentor from August 1991 to his death in April 1998

A Most Remarkable Man

To me Dr. Hall was a most remarkable man.
His life and work helped people to become the best that they can.
He studied the good in others and invested in their strengths
In pursuit of which he went to great lengths.

He invited people to become successful and significant.
And become better citizens.
So we need to respond to Dr. Hall's call and R.S.V.P.
By following his ways diligently.

First we need to build good Relationships, those which benefit all parties involved,
In which mutual trust is built and any problems resolved.
In so doing Dr. Hall's relationship law we most certainly will learn,
Namely, that when we invest in people for their sakes we always receive a hidden return.

Second there is his Strengths Investment Approach that we can deploy,
And use our strengths, which are the things we are good at and enjoy,
To bring out the strengths in others and see all parties grow.
Dr. Hall knew we would create a 'ripple-effect' which would be forever in flow.

He used top performers to mentor those with high potentiality
And achieved amazing results from this strategy.
According to Dr. Hall's approach the benefits of using strengths
needed to be explored,
When dealing with weaknesses, the most severe of which need to be
managed, not ignored,

Third we need to realize that we are the chief executive of the lives
we are living,
And become Vision, Value and Virtue driven.
To create big dreams, which are goals with wings,
Constantly aware that there is no right way to do the wrong things.

Fourth we need to adopt a Positive Approach and be optimistic.
Avoid becoming delusional Pollyannas, and always try to remain
realistic.
What we stand for the opposite we must be against.
For Dr. Hall cultivating positive feelings reduced stress and makes
most sense.

As part of his studies on how top performers think, feel and act,
It was necessary to find out how they how they responded not only
to setbacks

But to dysfunctional behaviors and to negativity,
And the ways they established harmony.

When asked what Dr. Hall considered to be his greatest professional achievement,
Without hesitation he said founding in 1949 the Nebraska Human Resources Foundation.*
Which is still thriving today, helping UNL graduates and Lincoln high school students become better citizens and stand tall.
The work of the Foundation is a lasting legacy for the most remarkable Dr. William E Hall.

*In 1956 the Foundation was formally incorporated as the Nebraska Human Resources Research Foundation (NHRRF). In 1988 the Foundation was renamed the Nebraska Human Resources Institute (NHRI) but the NHRRF has been retained as a not for profit unit related to NHRI.

An Ideal Citizen

Someone who thinks none harm,
   wills none harm,
   says none harm,
   does none harm.

Someone who in themselves feels warm,
   is to their neighbor warm,
   to their family and friends warm,
   to their enemies warm.

Someone whose inner light shines bright and takes
   delight in the sharing of their flame.
Someone who makes a difference –
   a candle lighting other candles –
Yet whose brilliance humbly remains the same.

Such people, are not mere
   citizens of our imagination.
They mingle among us and escape our due consideration.

Questions of Life and Love

What on earth is the real point of our birth?
To flourish what are we supposed to do?
To love and be loved for all we are worth?

Is there a purpose we are meant to serve?
What destination are we heading to?
What on earth is the point of our birth?

Is life over when we breathe our last breath?
How do we avoid feeling sad and blue?
To love and be loved for all we are worth?

What moral compass points to our last berth?
When to go solo, when part of a crew?
What on earth is the point of our birth?

Why do our kind kill for pieces of turf?
What can stop the pain war victims go through?
To love and be loved for all we are worth?

What do rich and poor folk truly deserve?
Can both become winners in our human zoo?
What on earth is the real point of our birth?
To love and be loved for all we are worth?

Pray Hear

Are you really there?
Are people talking to fresh air
When addressing you in prayer?

Is anybody home?
Are people talking to themselves
Or leaving messages on an imaginary answer phone?

Seriously, seriously,
Have you been trying to get through to me
Without making a forced entry?

If you really can't appear,
Then speak I am all ears.
But I've been listening for many years.

How do you relate?
I suppose I'll have to wait.
Time's passing, it's getting late.

If love is who you really are.
I don't have to go very far.
I can do that for sure.

Are you really there?
Am I just speaking to fresh air?
Pray, what is going on here?

United We Stand

Physicists are driven to explore the vastness of our universe,
And their telescopes, microscopes and colliders unearth strange events.
Is all this random or is the discovered order something quite terse,
An explanation we humans invent?

Are we God-created or stardust evolved from a primordial cloud?
Are we on earth to fulfil some proper purpose,
Or just members of an enigmatic crowd,
Clumsy clowns in a cruel cognitive circus?

Our universe is about things relating with each other.
Things are not always what they appear to be.
What fundamental laws can we uncover,
And reveal some of the mystery?

When others suffer we cannot call ourselves human,
If we do not feel their pain,
And reach out to help them.
Words without actions are somewhat in vain.

If humans are all part of the same being then united we stand,
And loving you and loving me are the same.
We can come thus come to understand,
That everybody ultimately gains.

Now or Never

How long does 'now' last?
When does the present become the past?
The hands on working clocks never stand still.
Is life a perpetual temporal treadmill?

Does 'now' reside in a twenty four hour day,
Clearly separated from yesterday,
Waiting for tomorrow to come,
As the earth orbits around the sun?

When we are told "to do it now" is a day too long?
If we think it is, we would be wrong.
It usually means "in this very instant."
Despite not being given a duration.

When does 'now' die and change into then?
When it changes to next is it born again?
Can 'now' ever be considered to be universal?
No need for clocks, no need for a journal!

Now at best is an approximation,
Related closely to a local situation.

It can be extended around the earth,
Although clocks differ in New York and Perth!

The universe is too vast to have a common present
Asking what is happening now on stars is a silly question.
When we look at the stars we are looking at the past.
The question is absurd and meaningless.

On earth, though vague, 'now' makes some sort of sense,
But when we use an astronomer's telescopic lens,
We have to choose whether,
It's 'now' or 'never.'

More or Less

The more knowledge we gain, more of the universe it shows.
Yet the circle of our ignorance grows.

Put another way – the more we know the more we don't know.
True humility comes to those who know that this is so.

When it comes to humility I must stress,
It's not thinking less of oneself, but thinking of oneself less.

Whole-ness

Reason expresses its points of view.
Feelings affect the way we think.
Both influence what we say and do.
Mind and actions inter-link.

Minds have biological roots,
Yet can produce surreal images.
Pink elephants in hobnailed boots.
In memory real horses pull real carriages.

We really are one integrated whole,
Able to generate ideas free from time and space,
With an all embracing role,
To make the human race race.

What's Our Life Coming To?

We can't live our lives over and change what we've done or said.
Yet the past has been buried partially alive, not totally dead.
In our memories there exist many a trace,
To help us run smarter through our human race.

Adding the fears of the future to the regrets of yesterday,
Would make our strongest falter and stumble on their way.
We need to hope for a better future and learn from the lessons of the past,
And build on a positive foundation and build something that will last.

It's up to us to decide what role we want to play,
And see if we can help others along their way.
Is it better to say "I'm okay and you're okay,"
And not put off 'till tomorrow what we could do today.

We could forgive offenders and accept forgiveness too,
Be more kind to others and estranged relationships renew.
Try to be more generous and remember to say "Thank you."
Rather than spending so much time paddling our own canoe.

Human Becomings

In line with the fundamental laws of physics and quantum mechanics,
Seeing humans as 'becomings' not 'beings' is not a matter of semantics.
We are happenings in a state of perpetual flux.
Reality is often counter-intuitive – not always the way it looks.

The present continuous is best seen as a permanent next,
The hands on a working clock are never ever fixed.
Our world is a network of ceaseless events and relations.
The fundamental laws of physics have no time in their equations.

Poets know the difficulty of putting human experience into words.
Scientists also struggle when the truth seems absurd.
As an adjective 'becoming' means 'attractively suitable,'
Which when related to humans, certainly fits the bill.

Acknowledgements

Many people, particularly family members, friends and mentors have in expressing their ideas and in living their lives been a positive influence. The most important of whom is Maureen, my better half, who has put up with me and inspired me for over fifty years. Her recommendations and suggestions have been invaluable. I also owe a debt of gratitude to my daughter, Larissa, who shields Maureen and me during the lockdown by doing our shopping and collecting prescriptions. In addition we have benefitted from her healing powers and medical knowledge, particularly in my case as I had two severe accidents which were not serious enough to use Accident and Emergency resources of the National Health Service. The first related to a twist in my right leg which severely sprained my right knee and ankle and in the short term prevented me from straightening my leg and caused a lot of swelling. The second related to a deep gash to my wedding-ring finger on my left hand when it was crushed between a spade and a concrete post as I was digging in the garden. Her massaging skills and holistic therapy soon put me well on the road to recovery as I can walk briskly again although my ankle is still slightly swollen and scar tissue is healing the finger wound without the need for any stitching. Not to forget that her greatest gift to us is our grandson Amir who was five years old in January 2020. It is a real pleasure to try to bring out the best in him and help him to bring out the best in others.

The late Dr. William E. Hall, my psychological mentor, was the first person who actively encouraged me to publish my verse and much of their content is derived from his example, teachings and vision.

Certainly Bob Attwood was instrumental in the germination of this collection.

Thank you all for all your help and inspiration.

Jim Meehan

About the Author

Jim Meehan was born in Liverpool, England, in the middle of the Second World War. During a career spanning fifty years, roughly half of which was spent in the British Motor Industry and half based in the United States operating as an international leadership consultant.

Designated a British Chartered Psychologist, a British Chartered Scientist, and a Chartered Fellow of the British Institute of Personnel and Development, he is also an Associate Member of the American Psychological Association.

Currently he lives in Solihull, England. His main interests lie in exploring the positive power human relationships have in bringing the best out of people and also delving into the interplay between thoughts, feelings and emotions and their role in the relief of pain.

Since his early childhood Meehan has been mesmerized by words in rhyme and for a hobby enjoys dabbling in verse. It was his psychological mentor Dr. William E. Hall who first encouraged him to publish his verse in the mid-nineties.

Unfortunately, due to the complications Of Type II Diabetes and poor blood circulation Meehan has had both legs amputated below the knee and is focusing on how to improve his mobility.

Printed in the United States
by Baker & Taylor Publisher Services